WE GATHER TOGETHER

We Gather Together

DAILY DEVOTIONALS FOR THANKSGIVING BASED ON THE HYMN, "WE GATHER TOGETHER."

Gwendolyn Harmon

Learning Ladyhood Press

Contents

Preface		1
1	To Ask	5
2	Gathering	7
3	Chastening	9
4	Hastening	11
5	His Will to Make Known	13
6	Oppressed, But Not Distressed	15
7	Never Forgotten	17
8	Beside to Guide	19
9	God With Us Joining	22
10	His Kingdom	24
11	Already Won	27
12	The Glory be Thine	29
13	The Triumph of our Leader	32
14	Our Defender	35
15	Tribulation	37
16	Praise and Petition	40

Copyright © 2021 by Gwendolyn Harmon

All rights reserved. No part of this book may be reproduced in any manner whatsoever without written permission except in the case of brief quotations embodied in critical articles and reviews.

First Printing, 2021

Cover photo by Rebecca Harmon, used with permission.

Preface

Thanksgiving is a wonderful holiday. As a child, I loved the smells of good things cooking in the kitchen, the sight of the special dishes on the table, and the sound of voices chattering in the living room after dinner. As an adult, I still enjoy the sights, smells, and sounds of Thanksgiving, but I now realize those things are not at all the primary reason we gather.

The United States of America has a remarkable national holiday which was established for the purpose of giving thanks to God for all that He has done for us. Our society, however, has shifted away from that focus, and in all the hype about parades and football, Black Friday deals and food, we can easily lose sight of the purpose of Thanksgiving. Even as a child, I would often get caught up in the preparations and time with family and completely forget to thank God for any of it.

My prayer for you as you read these devotionals is that your heart will be filled to overflowing with gratitude for all that God has done and continues to do on your behalf.

We Gather Together

We gather together to ask the Lord's blessing,
He chastens and hastens His will to make known;
The wicked oppressing now cease from distressing,
Sing praises to His name, He forgets not His own.

Beside us to guide us, our God with us joining,
Ordaining, maintaining His kingdom divine;
So from the beginning the fight we were winning,
Thou, Lord wast at our side: The glory be Thine!

We all do extol Thee, Thou Leader triumphant,
And pray that Thou still our Defender wilt be.
Let Thy congregation escape tribulation;
Thy name be ever praised: O Lord, make us free!

Theodore Baker

1

To Ask

"We gather together to ask the Lord's blessing"

I always used to take for granted the ability to gather with my family and friends, especially during a holiday. Always, that is, until the year my governor declared it illegal to gather. Suddenly, celebrating Thanksgiving with one's extended family became an act of rebellion, even a misdemeanor.

Perhaps you experienced something similar during the pandemic. I think the quarantines and restrictions have given Christians in America a taste of what many before us have suffered at the hands of anti-Christian governments, and what many today are suffering in many countries of the world where persecution of Christians is a daily occurrence.

This hymn, *We Gather Together*, was written in 1597 to celebrate Holland's newly-won freedom from Spain, at that time a strictly Catholic nation which had overrun their country, terrorizing and persecuting Protestant Christians throughout the land.

You'll notice the theme of God's deliverance throughout the hymn, but this first line suggests another facet to our American Thanksgiving gatherings. We gather, we eat, we celebrate, and hopefully we also remember to give thanks to God for His provision.

When the Christians in Holland gathered to celebrate their new independence and religious freedom, they were not just there to thank God, though that was part of it. They gathered to ask for the blessing of God on their new nation. I imagine their attitude would have been similar to that of our founding fathers during the formation of the United States.

You and I gather to give thanks and to *enjoy* God's blessings, but would it not be equally good to *ask* for God's continued blessing? As we gather this Thanksgiving, we can ask the blessing of God, not only on our feast and fellowship, but also on the days and months to come.

Have you asked for God's blessing today?

2

Gathering

We gather together to ask the Lord's blessing

Gathering is an essential part of our Thanksgiving celebration. When I was younger, we would have a whole houseful of people, and everyone would bring something delicious to add to the feast. The house was full of light and laughter, and everyone was on their best behavior… well, *most* of the time.

As the years have passed, our houseful became a handful, and then dwindled to just my parents and I and one aunt. Last Thanksgiving, I found myself moving the extra chairs away from the dining room table, and was suddenly struck by the remembrance of those years when we had to move those same chairs to the living room after Thanksgiving dinner so everyone could have a place to sit. It was a poignant memory that instantly transported me to times when the house was brimming with people. How sweet it had been to gather together with all those dear loved ones!

And yet, though I was missing the happy days of hosting a houseful, I was reminded that I did still have a family with whom to gather, even if only a few could come. There was still much for which to be thankful. Missing the days gone by didn't change the blessings God had for me that day or today. He is still present with me, and *He* is the source of all peace and joy.

So whether you are preparing for a houseful, a handful, or just yourself, remember that Jesus has said,

"lo, I am with you alway, even unto the end of the world." Matthew 28:20

To gather with family and friends is sweet, indeed, but to gather oneself close to the Lord is the sweetest fellowship of all!

Are you choosing to draw close to God today?

3

Chastening

He chastens and hastens His will to make known

Our list of things for which we are grateful usually doesn't include the word *chastening*. In fact, it is seldom used these days. Noah Webster's 1828 dictionary tells us that the word *chasten* means "to correct by punishment; to punish; to inflict pain for the purpose of reclaiming an offender." It also can mean, "to purify from faults and errors."

None of us like to feel we are being punished, even when it is for our good, but have you ever considered that the chastening of God is actually a blessing? Consider this passage from Psalm 94:

"Blessed is the man whom Thou chastenest, O Lord, and teachest him out of Thy law; That Thou mayest give him rest from the days of adversity, until the pit be digged for the wicked. For the Lord will not cast off His people, neither will He forsake His inheritance. But judgment shall return unto righteousness: and all the upright in heart shall follow it." (12-15)

The reason God chastens His children is to teach us to do right, so that we might have peace and rest. It is not pleasant to be chastened, but the results are always for our good. Hebrews 12:11 sums this up well:

> *"Now no chastening for the present seemeth to be joyous, but grievous: nevertheless afterward it yieldeth the peaceable fruit of righteousness unto them which are exercised thereby."*

Chastening is also a reminder of our position as a child of God:

> *"And ye have forgotten the exhortation which speaketh unto you as unto children, My son, despise not thou the chastening of the Lord, nor faint when thou art rebuked of Him: For whom the Lord loveth He chasteneth, and scourgeth every son whom He receiveth. If ye endure chastening, God dealeth with you as with sons; for what son is he whom the father chasteneth not?" (Hebrews 12: 5-7)*

Just like a good parent will discipline his or her child from a heart of love that wants to protect and help that child learn to do right, so God chastens us, disciplining His children with a heart of love that wants to reconcile, restore, and protect.

What "chastening" is the Holy Spirit drawing your attention to today? Will you choose to thank Him for it?

4

Hastening

He chastens and hastens His will to make known

It is strange to think of God doing anything with what we call haste. He is eternal, existing outside of time, yet there are two occasions when God describes Himself as *hastening*. The first is in the book of Isaiah, at the end of a passage detailing the glorious future God has planned, both for Israel *and* for each of us New Testament believers, since the following description from Isaiah matches that given in Revelation 22 of the heavenly New Jerusalem.

> *"The sun shall be no more thy light by day; neither for brightness shall the moon give light unto thee: but the Lord shall be unto thee an everlasting light, and thy God thy glory. Thy sun shall no more go down; neither shall thy moon withdraw itself: for the Lord shall be thine everlasting light, and the days of thy mourning shall be ended. Thy people also shall be all righteous: they shall inherit the land for ever, the branch of My planting, the work of My hands, that I may be glorified. A little one shall become a thousand, and a small one a strong nation: I the Lord will hasten it in his time."*
> (Isaiah 60:19-22)

God's "hastening" is seen here in perspective. He will hasten it *in his time*, or when it is time for it to happen. When God has promised to do something, He always keeps His promise, and always at just the right moment.

The other instance of God using the word *hasten* to describe His actions is found in Jeremiah's first conversation with God, in which God informs Jeremiah that he had been chosen before birth to carry God's message to His people. Jeremiah eventually voices his feelings of inadequacy, and God promises to be with him and help him. Then God shows him a vision of an almond branch (perhaps a reminder of Aaron's rod that budded and bloomed and bore fruit, as a symbol of his God-given authority.)

> *"Moreover the word of the Lord came unto me, saying, Jeremiah, what seest thou? And I said, I see a rod of an almond tree.*
> *Then said the Lord unto me, Thou hast well seen: for I will hasten My word to perform it." (Jeremiah 1:11-12)*

Again, we see God promising to hasten to perform that which He has spoken. We can be sure that God will do as He has said, at just the right time. He will not delay or drag His feet: He will act when it is time.

This is a blessed truth for us to remember as we approach this season of remembering all that God has done for us. How deserving God is of our thankfulness, even just for these two details of His character: that He is trustworthy and timely. He will do as He has promised, and at just the right moment.

Can you think of an instance where God has worked in your life at just the right moment? Stop and thank Him for never being late!

5

His Will to Make Known

He chastens and hastens His will to make known

As a Christian, I am always trying to find God's will for my everyday decisions. Occasionally, I find myself complaining that I just can't figure out what God's will is. In these moments, I'm usually focused on making my decision and getting it over with. But my impatience with the lack of clear, immediate leading is merely an indication of my unwillingness to yield to the will of God if it means I must *wait* to make my decision.

The truth is, God has given us an entire book devoted to communicating His will to us. The Bible may not specifically tell me which car I should buy or what I should wear today, but it does promise that God gives wisdom to those who ask *(James 1:5)* and that if I walk in the Spirit, I will not fulfill the lusts of the flesh. *(Galatians 5:16)*

There are many clear, direct statements about God's will throughout Scripture, but one, in particular, stands out during this season:

> *"In every thing give thanks: for this is the will of God in Christ Jesus concerning you."* (1 Thessalonians 5:18)

We often assume that God's will for us will match up with ours: that if we are obeying God and living for Him, life will be smooth and easy, but that is not necessarily the case. In fact, we are told that

> *"all that live godly in Christ Jesus shall suffer persecution."* (2 Timothy 3:12)

As much as we dislike it, suffering is a part of the Christian life: a part of God's will for us. So what do we do when suffering comes? 1 Peter 4:19 tells us:

> *"Wherefore let them that suffer according to the will of God commit the keeping of their souls to Him in well doing, as unto a faithful Creator."*

The command to give thanks *always* for *all things* includes these areas of suffering according to God's will. We never enjoy suffering, but we can give thanks for it nonetheless if we keep our eyes on the faithfulness of our Creator, who works all things for our good and His glory.

What is there in your life that you have a hard time thanking God for? Will you choose to give thanks for it today?

6

Oppressed, But Not Distressed

The wicked oppressing, now cease from distressing

As we have already noted, this song was written in celebration of Holland's national independence as well as religious freedom. In their case, the wicked oppressors had been defeated and could not distress them any more.

This line reminds me of a precious truth from the life of Paul. 2 Corinthians 4 paints a picture for us of the true nature of the Christian life.

"We are troubled on every side, yet not distressed; we are perplexed but not in despair; Persecuted, but not forsaken; cast down, but not destroyed; Always bearing about in the body the dying of the Lord Jesus, that the life also of Jesus might be made manifest in our body." (8-10)

You see, the most wicked oppressor can never take away the joy of our salvation. In fact, throughout history, persecuted Christians have exhibited a more radiant joy than is common among those of us who find ourselves living in easier circumstances.

The wicked cannot take away the Christian's joy: but the Christian can give it up by allowing the oppression of the wicked to shift their focus. Just like Peter walking to Jesus on the water, we need to keep our eyes on Jesus in order to stay above the waves of worry that crash about us in this world. If we allow ourselves to fix our gaze on the wicked, we will become consumed with worry instead of filled with faith. We will be overwhelmed by distress and despair and will no longer shine the light of Christ's joy, hope, and peace to the world around us.

Instead, we must fix our eyes on Jesus and choose to trust Him, no matter what is happening in the world around us. We must refuse to become distracted with thoughts of worry or imaginings of what the future may hold.

Romans 8:38-39 helps reset our perspective:

"For I am persuaded, that neither death, nor life, nor angels, nor principalities, nor powers, nor things present, nor things to come, Nor height, nor depth, nor any other creature shall be able to separate us from the love of God, which is in Christ Jesus our Lord."

In what areas of your life does the Holy Spirit want to reset your focus today?

7

Never Forgotten

Sing praises to His name! He forgets not His own

Isaiah 44 begins with God calling Israel back to Him, expressing the majesty of who He is, and assuring them that they are His. God then denounces Israel's idolatry, describing how ridiculous it is to trust in a piece of wood, or stone, or metal. He paints a verbal picture of a man growing a tree and then cutting it down to use the wood for his fire, saving part of it to make into an idol to worship.

The people had forgotten the God who loved them, to whom they belonged, and instead gave the worship of which only He is worthy to inanimate things *they themselves had made!* In fact, when faced with an invading army only the one true God could stop, they turned instead to these same idols, trusting them for deliverance and protection.

In the midst of all this foolishness and sin, God reminds Israel of an important truth:

"Remember these, O Jacob and Israel; for thou art My servant: I have formed thee; thou art My servant; O Israel, thou shalt not be forgotten of Me. I have blotted out, as a thick cloud, thy sins: return unto Me; for I have redeemed thee." (vv.21-22)

Israel had forgotten God, but God had not forgotten Israel. It's the same with you and me. God is holy and just, and thus our sin separates us from Him, but He never forgets us. His arms are always open to His children, waiting to forgive and restore.

What more fitting response can there be than that which God Himself gives in the very next verse:

"Sing, O ye heavens; for the Lord hath done it: shout, ye lower parts of the earth: break forth into singing, ye mountains, O forest, and every tree therein: for the Lord hath redeemed Jacob, and glorified Himself in Israel."(v.23)

The rest of the chapter is a declaration of God's power and faithfulness. It is hard to do Isaiah 44 justice in summary, so I recommend you set this book down and go read the whole chapter for yourself. Then see if the truths of God's character and love don't make you want to break out in singing in praise of His name!

> ***God will not forget you. Does that truth move your heart to praise Him?***

8

Beside to Guide

Beside us to guide us, Our God with us joining

John 14-17 is packed with comforting and encouraging truths. These chapters comprise what theologians call the Olivet Discourse, the teachings Jesus spoke to his disciples the night He was arrested. Within these chapters, Jesus speaks much of going away and sending the Holy Spirit to comfort us. In chapter 14, Jesus says,

"But the Comforter, which is the Holy Ghost, whom the Father will send in My name, He shall teach you all things, and bring all things to your remembrance, whatsoever I have said unto you." (v.26)

This is yet another glorious truth for which we ought to be filled with gratitude to God. The constant presence of the Holy Spirit dwelling inside us is one of the most foundational blessings of the Christian life. The Holy Spirit bears witness of our salvation (Romans 8:16), intercedes on our behalf when we do not know just how to pray about a particular situation (Romans 8:26), distributes spiritual gifts (1 Corinthians 12:8-11), and changes us to be more and more like Christ

(2 Corinthians 3:18). The Holy Spirit also guides us into all truth (John 16:13).

Jesus' last words to His disciples before He ascended into heaven give us another glimpse of what the Holy Spirit does through us:

> *"But ye shall receive power, after that the Holy Ghost is come upon you: and ye shall be witnesses unto Me both in Jerusalem, and in all Judaea, and in Samaria, and unto the uttermost part of the earth." (Acts 1:8)*

The Holy Spirit gives us the power to bear witness of Jesus' death, burial, and resurrection. Jesus sends His followers out to tell others about Him, yet He does not send us alone. Matthew 28:19-20 says,

> *"Go ye therefore, and teach all nations, baptizing them in the name of the Father, and of the Son, and of the Holy Ghost: Teaching them to observe all things whatsoever I have commanded you: and lo, I am with you always, even unto the end of the world. Amen."*

We are promised both the power and the presence of God as we go out to reach others with the gospel. In Mark 13, Jesus tells His disciples to expect persecution, saying,

> *"But when they shall lead you, and deliver you up, take no thought beforehand what ye shall speak, neither do ye premeditate: but whatsoever shall be given you in that hour, that speak ye: for it is not ye that speak, but the Holy Ghost." (v.11)*

The Holy Spirit will even give us just the right words to speak at just the right moment. While it is important to know God's Word (so the Holy Spirit can help us by bringing it to mind), we don't need to have every word planned out in advance in order to share Christ.

In fact, this passage indicates that we ought just to trust God to bring the words to mind as we need them!

The indwelling presence of the Holy Spirit is not just a promise: it is a reality. And the promise of power and guidance as we witness is just as true for us today as it was for the disciples.

Thank God for His guidance and power!
How is the Holy Spirit guiding you to share Christ with others today?

9

God With Us Joining

Beside us to guide us, our God with us joining

This is one of the astounding things about the Christian life. As the saved in Christ, we are workers together with Him *(2 Corinthians 6:1)*. The same God who gave us the precious gift of salvation now allows us to serve as His ambassadors *(2 Corinthians 5:20)*. We are to represent Christ to the world, and yet, we are not left to do it alone. Paul tells us in 1 Corinthians 15:10,

> *"But by the grace of God I am what I am: and His grace which was bestowed upon me was not in vain; but I laboured more abundantly than they all: yet not I, but the grace of God which was with me."*

You see, God gives us His grace with which to do our work. It is through God's power, God's wisdom, and God's enablement that we are able to do anything for Him. As we move to do His will, He joins with us, giving us all we need to accomplish the things He has called us to do. I am always encouraged by this truth in 1 Thessalonians 5:24:

> *"Faithful is He that calleth you, who also will do it."*

It is God who does the work: but He does it *through* you and me. Galatians 2:20 explains,

> *"I am crucified with Christ: nevertheless I live; yet not I, but Christ liveth in me: and the life which I now live in the flesh I live by the faith of the Son of God, who loved me, and gave Himself for me."*

As we obey God's Word and the promptings of the Holy Spirit, God works both in and through us for His glory and our good. We live our lives, but we can only live in obedience to God with His help, His enabling.

What does God want to do in and through you today?

10

His Kingdom

Ordaining, maintaining His kingdom Divine

When Jesus first began preaching and teaching, His message was simple:

"Repent: for the kingdom of heaven is at hand." (Matthew 4:17)

If you search in a concordance or on a Bible app for verses containing the word *kingdom* in the gospels, you will notice that from the start, Jesus' kingdom was of a different nature than the kingdoms of this world.

In the hours leading up to the crucifixion, Pilate asked Jesus if He was the king of the Jews. John 18:36 records His response:

"My kingdom is not of this world: if My kingdom were of this world, then would My servants fight, that I should not be delivered to the Jews: but now is My kingdom not from hence."

The kingdom of God is unlike any other kingdom. The Pharisees asked Jesus one day when the kingdom of God was going to come. He explained,

"The kingdom of God cometh not with observation: Neither shall they say, Lo here! or, lo there! for, behold, the kingdom of God is within you." (Luke 17:20-21)

The kingdom of God is the inheritance of those who have trusted Christ as Savior. With such a magnificent future ahead of us, we should live each day as Colossians 1 says,

"Giving thanks unto the Father, which hath made us meet to be partakers of the inheritance of the saints in light: Who hath delivered us from the power of darkness, and hath translated us into the kingdom of His dear Son: In whom we have redemption through His blood, even the forgiveness of sins: Who is the image of the invisible God, the firstborn of every creature: For by Him were all things created, that are in heaven, and that are in earth, visible and invisible, whether they be thrones, or dominions, or principalities or powers: all things were created by Him, and for Him: And He is before all things, and by Him all things consist." (1:12-17)

This passage reminds us that the kingdom of God was indeed ordained and is every moment maintained by God. It is not earthly, but Divine. It is an everlasting kingdom that shall have no end. *(Luke 1:33)*

Just as Abraham did, you and I look *"for a city which hath foundations, whose builder and maker is God" (Hebrews 11:10)* There will come a day when the kingdoms of this world will *"become the kingdoms of our Lord, and of His Christ," (Revelation 11:15)* and the kingdom of God to which the saved in Christ belong will be both spiritual and physical.

Until then, we each have a responsibility as Christians to *"walk worthy of God, who hath called you into His kingdom and glory."* (1 Thessalonians 2:12)

How does God want you to "walk worthy" today?

11

Already Won

So from the beginning the fight we were winning

The book of John begins with the beautiful words,

"In the beginning was the Word, and the Word was with God, and the Word was God. The same was in the beginning with God." (John 1:1-2)

In the very beginning, before the world was made, God the Son existed with God the Father and God the Holy Spirit. The one triune God worked in perfect harmony to form the world and its inhabitants. I love to read the creation account and marvel at the magnificent power of God, Who could create the world just by speaking.

Later on, in the book of Revelation, Jesus is described as, *"the Lamb slain from the foundation of the world." (13:8)*

You see, even before Adam and Eve sinned, God knew it was coming. Being eternal, He exists outside of time, and being omniscient, He knows all that has ever happened or will ever happen. Jesus did step into history *"in due time,"* as Romans 5:6 describes it.

Christ suffered and died at a specific time and place to pay the penalty for our sin, but in the sight of God, it was as if Jesus had already sacrificed Himself for us when the world was first formed.

It's hard to wrap our minds around, but it's true. God's plan has always been that the gift of salvation be offered to mankind. It is no accident that Genesis 3, which contains the description of the first sin, also contains the first promise of a Savior.

In this way, it is true that "from the beginning the fight we were winning." Christ is our source of victory, a victory won by our eternal God before the world was ever formed.

As we prepare for the upcoming day of giving thanks to God, it is good for us to think upon the glorious truth of victory in Christ. This truth is not just an abstract idea, though. It is meant to encourage us to be strong in the Lord, and to live victoriously through His power:

"But thanks be to God, which giveth us the victory through our Lord Jesus Christ. Therefore, my beloved brethren, be ye stedfast, unmoveable, always abounding in the work of the Lord, forasmuch as ye know that your labour is not in vain in the Lord." (1 Corinthians 15:57-58)

How does the truth of Christ's victory encourage you to live victoriously today?

12

The Glory be Thine

Thou, Lord, wast at our side:
The glory be Thine!

The hymn-writer was looking back over an arduous time of literal fighting for the freedom to worship God. As he looked back, he saw that God was the source of their victory. This whole stanza expresses the idea that the victory belongs to God, not to them. It reminds me of Psalm 124:

"If it had not been the Lord who was on our side, now may Israel say; If it had not been the Lord who was on our side, when men rose up against us: Then they had swallowed us up quick, when their wrath was kindled against us: Then the waters had overwhelmed us, the stream had gone over our soul: Then the proud waters had gone over our soul. Blessed be the Lord, who hath not given us as a prey to their teeth. Our soul is escaped as a bird out of the snare of the fowlers: the snare is broken, and we are escaped. Our help is in the name of the Lord, who made heaven and earth."

This psalm is one of the "songs of ascent" sung during the yearly journey up to Jerusalem to celebrate the Passover. It is a psalm of David, a man who saw God's deliverance firsthand many times over his life, in both physical, political, and spiritual battles.

Israel, too, could collectively remember many instances of God's deliverance; and this psalm was not just an expression of gratefulness for the past, but also a reminder that God was still needed as their source of help in the present and the future.

This hymn expresses the same idea. If had not been for the Lord's help, the Protestant Christians in Holland fighting for their very existence would surely have fallen to the ruthless strength of their Spanish enemies.

The anonymous writer who penned these words certainly had cause to rejoice with grateful heart, as David did, for the obvious Divine help which had brought them safely through the conflict and gained their freedom and independence. But the nation still needed God's help, if it was to retain its freedom.

The same is true for us in our daily lives. Were it not for the Lord, we would not be able to have victory over sin, daily living out the truth that Christ has made us free. *(Romans 8:2)* This is why we are admonished to:

"Stand fast therefore in the liberty wherewith Christ hath made us free, and be not entangled again with the yoke of bondage." (Galatians 5:1)

If we rely on our own strength, we will inevitably become *"entangled again with the yoke of bondage."* Instead, we must yield to the Holy Spirit, trusting Him to help us. Only then can we live the lives God desires us to live. As Jesus said,

"Without Me, ye can do nothing" (John 15:5)

In what ways have you seen God's hand of deliverance in your life in the past? How does He want to deliver you today as you walk in the Spirit?

13

The Triumph of our Leader

We all do extol Thee,
Thou Leader, Triumphant,

As we have seen, the Christians in Holland acknowledged God as the One who had led them to that moment of victory. Although you and I may not find ourselves fighting any physical battles today, it is important for us to remember, as the hymn-writer reminds us, that God is *our* triumphant leader also.

It is easy to give intellectual assent to the truth that God has already won the victory over sin and death and hell, but when was the last time you stopped to gaze upon Him in all His triumphant glory?

Scripture gives us many opportunities to do this, whether it is in the accounts of the resurrection or of God majestically intervening on Israel's behalf to defeat their enemies or in the many prophetic passages describing God in all His triumphant glory.

One of my favorites is this little glimpse into the celebration of God's triumph in Revelation 19:

> *"And after these things I heard a great voice of much people in heaven, saying, Alleluia; Salvation, and glory, and honour, and power, unto the Lord our God: For true and righteous are His judgements: for He hath judged the great whore, which did corrupt the earth with her fornication, and hath avenged the blood of His servants at her hand. And again they said, Alleluia. And her smoke rose up for ever and ever. And the four and twenty elders and the four beasts fell down and worshipped God that sat on the throne, saying, Amen; Alleluia. And a voice came out of the throne, saying, Praise our God, all ye His servants, and ye that fear Him, both small and great. And I heard as it were the voice of a great multitude, and as the voice of many waters, and as the voice of mighty thunderings, saying, Alleluia: for the Lord God omnipotent reigneth." (Revelation 19:1-6)*

It is easy to forget that God is the Just Judge; but He is, and one day He will set everything right. No one truly "gets away" with anything in this world, because God knows all, sees all, and is omnipotent and just.

But what strikes me about this passage as I read it today is the awe-inspiring fact that one day, you and I will stand with all the rest of the saved in Christ and praise God with those exact words. –I wonder if we will suddenly realize that the scene seems familiar, and rejoice all the more that the day of triumph and rejoicing we read about and longed for all those years has finally come to pass!

That day has not come, but it will. When we are tempted to be discouraged, we can remember that we are following the leading of the just and holy God who has already proven His victory over sin and death and will one day bring all things to a final triumphant conclusion.

> *What does the reminder that God is our triumphant Leader mean in your heart and life today?*

14

Our Defender

And pray that Thou still our Defender wilt be.

Does it ever seem odd to you to pray for something God has already promised? I used to wonder if it was really okay to ask God to do things for us if He had already said He would, but I have noticed in recent years just how many times throughout the Bible godly men and women do just that. The hymn-writer also does this. As we sing this hymn with our fellow believers, we ask for God to be our Defender in the future as He has been in the past. As Hebrews 13 reminds us,

> *"for He hath said, I will never leave thee, nor forsake thee. So that we may boldly say, the Lord is my helper, and I will not fear what man shall do unto me." (vv.5-6)*

So we know that God will not leave us, and we need not fear what men can do, for God is with us. So why do we ask that He will still be our Defender? It's not to remind God of what He has said, for He never forgets. He is omniscient, which means He knows all things, and He is immutable, which means He can never change; so forgetting something He promised is certainly out of the question.

So what is it about? What is the purpose of asking for something we already have? This is one of the many occasions when prayer is more for the purpose of changing *us* than it is about changing the thing we are praying about.

You see, as we pray for God to be our Defender, we necessarily yield to the truth that we *need* a Defender. It brings us face to face with the reality of our helplessness and God's infinite ability and willingness to be our Help.

The act of asking, even when we have already been promised the thing we are asking for, also helps us take ownership of the results. In other words, it is easier to trust that God will help you when you have asked Him to before and seen Him faithfully follow through. Asking God for that which He has promised is essentially a way to build our faith.

This hymn is intended to be sung congregationally. This is significant as well in this area of praying for God to be our Defender. When we come together as a group to ask something, it not only strengthens our faith *individually*, it also strengthens our *corporate* faith. It gives the group as a whole something to point to, a common experience of God's faithfulness to remind each other of when trials come. It also builds our sense of unity in Christ and knits our hearts to each other.

Whether corporately or individually, there is great value in asking God for what He has already promised. And, besides, we already know what the answer to those prayers will be!

What is God prompting you to ask Him today?

15

Tribulation

Let Thy congregation escape tribulation

When I think of the word *tribulation*, I think of God's post-rapture season of pouring out His judgment on the earth. I somehow don't think that is what the hymn-writer is referring to in this stanza, though. From the context, it does not seem as though his focus is eschatological, that is, dealing with events still to come.

Rather, I think he is using the word in its most literal sense to refer to the persecutions the Christians in Holland had just gone through. They had just come out of a time of severe tribulation and were not eager to have the painful experience repeated. Persecution is a normal part of the Christian life, as 2 Timothy 3:12 points out,

> "Yea, and all that will live godly in Christ Jesus shall suffer persecution."

Though it is sometimes the case, the inevitable persecution spoken of in 2 Timothy is not limited to a broad governmental level of society. It could be a neighbor, coworker, or family member who is not pleased that you are following Christ. We are to respond to persecution by exhibiting a Christlike character, whatever form the persecution takes.

But the inevitability of persecution does not mean it's wrong to pray that God's people may avoid the kind of conflict the Christians in Holland went through. We know this because 1 Timothy tells us,

> *"I exhort, therefore, that, first of all, supplications, prayers, intercessions, and giving of thanks, be made for all men; For kings, and for all that are in authority; that we may lead a quiet and peaceable life in all godliness and honesty. For this is good and acceptable in the sight of God our Savior; Who will have all men to be saved, and come unto the knowledge of the truth."*
> *(2:1-4)*

Notice that we are to pray and give thanks for those in authority over us *so that* we can lead quiet, peaceable lives for the furthering of the gospel. It is not wrong to pray for God's people to have the peace and freedom to openly share the gospel.

The United States of America was founded on the principles of religious freedom. According to our Constitution, we are still free to share the gospel without fear of punishment. Of course, America is not perfect, and Christians *are* being persecuted in various ways; but we still have the freedom to tell others about Jesus, so that they, too can *"come unto the knowledge of the truth." (2 Timothy 2:4)*

Part of the responsibility that comes with that freedom is to pray for our leaders, that they would make righteous decisions that promote peace and the free spread of the gospel.

Have you prayed and given thanks for your leaders today? Are you using your freedom to live a quiet and peacable life for the furtherance of the gospel?

16

Praise and Petition

Thy name be ever praised:
O, Lord, make us free!

The people of Holland no doubt gathered and sang this hymn from hearts of grateful praise to God as they gathered to celebrate their newly won independence. For us today, it serves as a reminder that the God who has been His people's help and defender in the past is still the same today.

We, too, can raise our hearts and voices in grateful praise to God, not just for His goodness to the Christians of Holland so long ago, but to us today as well. As we celebrate Thanksgiving with our families, praise should be on our hearts and lips, corporately and individually.

But the hymn-writer does not end with praise. He raises one last pleading cry to the Lord, a cry for freedom. Whether it is the religious freedom on a national level, or the spiritual freedom we enjoy in Christ, the fact remains the same: these freedoms only benefit us if we use them. The freedom we have in the United States to worship God and to evangelize the lost must be exercised if it is to make any difference.

Likewise, the freedom we enjoy in Christ is ours every moment, but only affects our lives if we *act* on it.

As we celebrate and give thanks for all that God has done for us, let us also remember to live each day in light of those blessings. This Thanksgiving, add to your grateful praises the hymn-writer's plea, and then do as Galatians 5:1 commands us:

"Stand fast therefore in the liberty wherewith Christ hath made us free"

How will you "stand fast" in liberty today?

www.ingramcontent.com/pod-product-compliance
Lightning Source LLC
Chambersburg PA
CBHW062206100526
44589CB00014B/1977